NATIONAL GEOGRAPHIC

Ladders

MOVING INTO THE FUTURE

Cars of the Future

Hit the Gas

How do you get from place to place? You might walk, ride your bike, or take a car or bus. There are many cars and trucks on the road today. Gas prices are soaring, so people want vehicles that use less gas or no gas. **Transportation** options are starting to change. Researchers are focusing on cars and fuels that are better for the environment and may save us money!

Surprisingly, for over a century, scientists have been experimenting with vehicles that do not run on gasoline. Around 1900, nearly one-third of all cars in big cities were electric cars, but people wanted more powerful, faster cars that could travel longer distances. Gas was cheap and easy to get in the early 1900s. So cars with gas-powered **internal combustion engines** were the best option. Most people still drive gas-powered cars. But that is starting to change.

Most cars on the highway use gas to fuel internal combustion engines.

Are Here!

by Stephanie Herbek

Gas Prices: Then and Now

Year	1930	1950	1970	1990	2000	2010	2011
Average Price per Gallon of Regular Unleaded	$0.17	$0.25	$0.50	$1.16	$2.35	$2.76	$3.50

Internal Combustion Engine: How It Works

When you turn the key in a gas-powered vehicle, electricity flows from the car battery to the motor and cranks the engine. Sparks ignite the fuel, which make pistons inside the engine move up and down. This activates the fuel pump, which pulls gas into the engine. As the pistons move, they turn the crankshaft and provide power to the transmission, which moves the car.

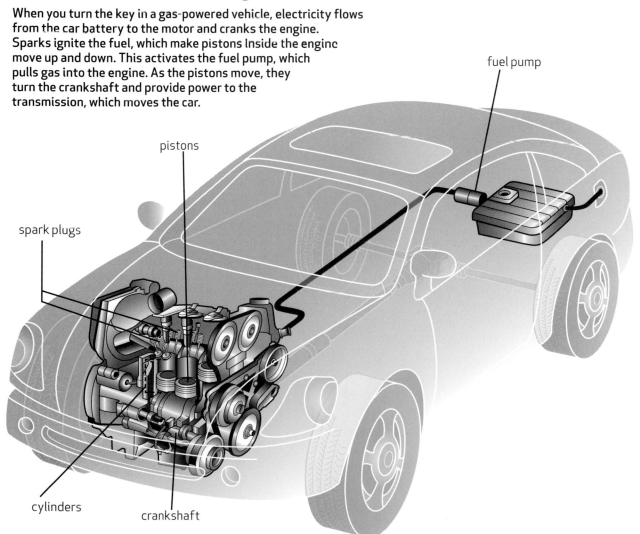

fuel pump

pistons

spark plugs

cylinders

crankshaft

Two in One

In science, a **hybrid** is a combination of two different things. In the car world, a hybrid is a vehicle that uses a small, gas-efficient engine plus a battery-powered electric motor. Hybrids pollute less and are cheaper to operate than gas-powered cars. They are an **innovation** in the car world.

The first hybrid passenger car was introduced in 1997. Early hybrids were expensive and slow compared to gas-powered cars. But these vehicles have improved. Today, most carmakers offer hybrid vehicles. And the number of hybrids produced each year is increasing.

Hybrid city buses are a common sight in the U.S., Europe, Scandinavia, and Canada.

Sleek body designs and lightweight materials help hybrids move efficiently.

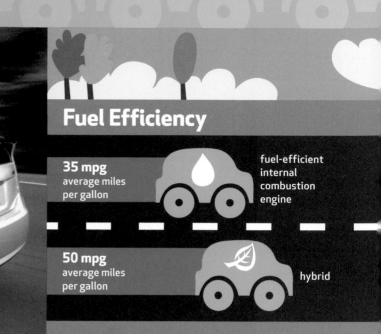

Fuel Efficiency

35 mpg
average miles
per gallon

fuel-efficient internal combustion engine

50 mpg
average miles
per gallon

hybrid

Hybrid: How It Works

Rechargeable batteries provide some of the energy needed to run hybrid cars. The batteries charge as the car runs. The gas engine of this hybrid shuts off when the car comes to a stop. The car's electric motor and batteries help restart the car when it's time to move.

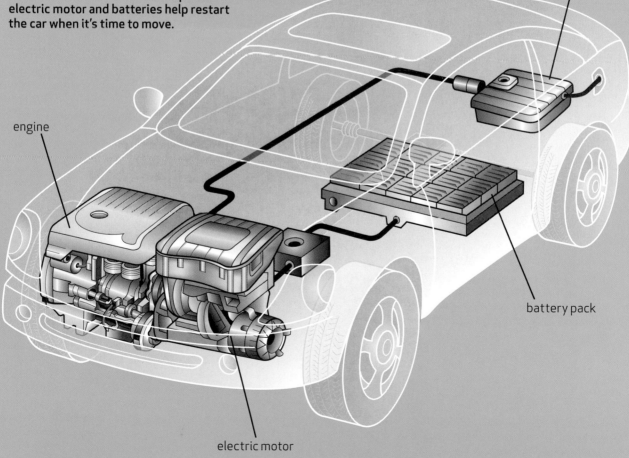

gas tank

engine

battery pack

electric motor

Plug It In

An electric vehicle, or "EV," is powered by a battery or a fuel cell. It gets its energy from electricity. Owners plug their EV into an electrical power source or neighborhood charging station. Some EVs have a gasoline tank. Gasoline is only used as a back up fuel.

EVs aren't perfect. They are more expensive than similar gas-powered cars and hybrids. They cannot travel as far as gas-powered cars without needing to be recharged. Additionally, it can take up to eight hours to fully charge some EV batteries. This is much slower than filling up a gas tank.

Thomas Edison is shown here with an electric vehicle in 1913. He believed the cars of the future would run on electricity.

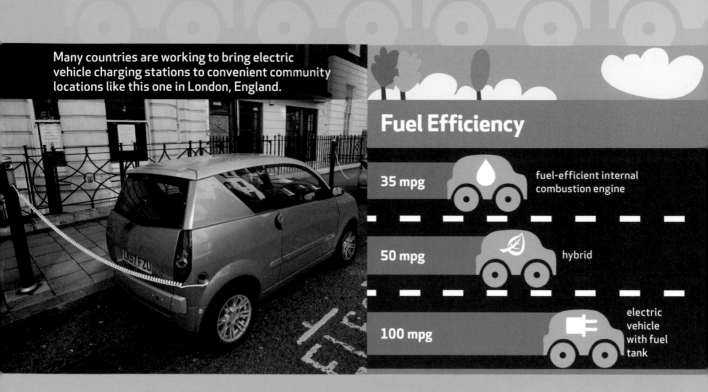

Many countries are working to bring electric vehicle charging stations to convenient community locations like this one in London, England.

Fuel Efficiency

35 mpg		fuel-efficient internal combustion engine
50 mpg		hybrid
100 mpg		electric vehicle with fuel tank

Electric Vehicle: How It Works

EVs are "fueled" by electricity alone. Owners plug their car into an electrical source, such as a charging station to charge its batteries. The batteries power the motor. Scientists are trying to develop smaller, lighter batteries that can recharge more quickly.

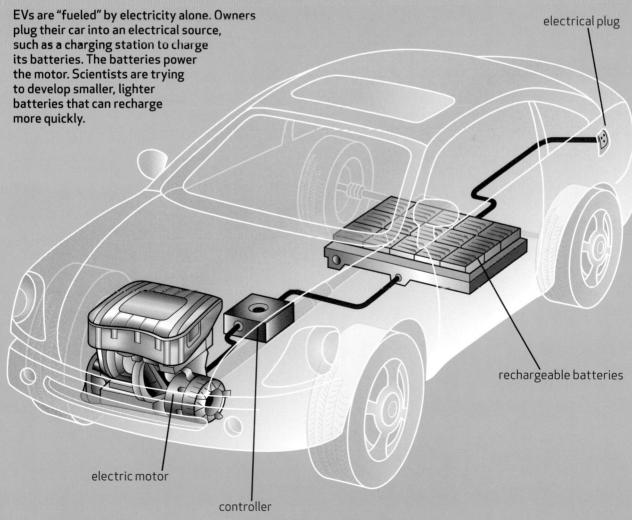

electrical plug

rechargeable batteries

electric motor

controller

Home-Grown and Deep-Fried

Fill it up! This phrase used to mean, "Fill up the car's tank with petroleum gasoline."

Gasoline and diesel fuel made from petroleum come from fossil fuels. Fossil fuels are pumped out of the ground. But cars can also use other types of fuels, such a **biofuels.** Biofuels are fuels made from materials we can grow, such as plants. Ethanol and biodiesel are two of the most common biofuels used today.

Ethanol is made from crops, such as corn. It is used in place of gasoline. Biodiesel is made from vegetable oil or animal fats. It is used in place of diesel fuel. Ethanol and biodiesel produce less pollution than petroleum fuels. And they are easy to produce. Many countries depend on fossil fuels. Making and using biofuels would allow countries to use less fossil fuels.

Vegetable oil used for fuel must first be filtered.

Cars that run on diesel fuel can also run on vegetable oil fuel.

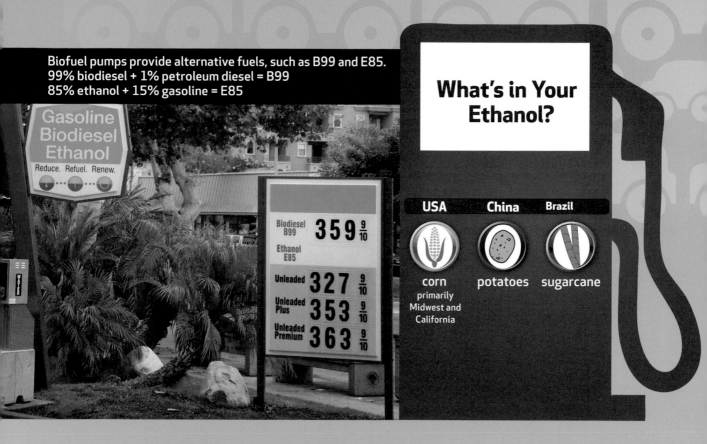

Biofuel pumps provide alternative fuels, such as B99 and E85.
99% biodiesel + 1% petroleum diesel = B99
85% ethanol + 15% gasoline = E85

Gasoline
Biodiesel
Ethanol
Reduce. Refuel. Renew.

Biodiesel B99	359 9/10
Ethanol E85	
Unleaded	327 9/10
Unleaded Plus	353 9/10
Unleaded Premium	363 9/10

What's in Your Ethanol?

USA	China	Brazil
corn	potatoes	sugarcane
primarily Midwest and California		

Vegetable Oil as Fuel: How It Works

Diesel fuel starts the car's engine. The engine heats the vegetable oil in the tank. When the oil is warm, the car begins running on vegetable oil instead of diesel fuel. When the car stops, the engine switches back to diesel fuel so it can start again.

vegetable oil tank

diesel fuel tank

engine

oil filter

Hydrogen Fueled

Hydrogen-powered vehicles may be the future of transportation. These vehicles use electricity from fuel cells. In a fuel cell, hydrogen is combined with oxygen. This produces electricity that powers the vehicle. Hydrogen cars produce water and heat. They do not pollute. Today there are few hydrogen filling stations. And fuel cells are expensive to build. But researchers are still working to improve this important **technology.**

Hydrogen-powered buses are in use in Reykjavik, Iceland.

The Pros and Cons of Green Vehicles

	Pro	Con
Hybrid vehicle	• Improved gas mileage • Reduced pollution	• More expensive than most gas-only vehicles • Slower acceleration than gas-only vehicles
Electric vehicle	• Very efficient • Minimal or no pollution	• Shorter driving range between charges than other types of vehicles • Long recharging time
Vegetable oil-fueled vehicle	• Plenty of biomass available to produce fuel • Less pollution than gas-powered vehicles	• Fewer miles per gallon than gasoline • Car modifications needed • Vegetable oil fuel not certified by EPA
Hydrogen-fueled vehicle	• Zero emissions • Less dependency on fossil fuel	• Still in the experimental stages • Few hydrogen stations available for refueling

What's the future of energy technology for transportation? Ethanol? Electricity? Hydrogen? It will certainly be different from the technology of today. And it will certainly affect our planet.

Check In What green vehicle would you choose? Why?

Moving Across, Below, and Up!

by John Manos

Human beings have always strived to overcome **limitations**. We have always been trying to move farther, faster, higher, and deeper. We want to do more than our bodies are able to do.

Throughout history, humans have wanted better **transportation**. We don't have wings to fly like birds or gills to swim like fish. Our bodies hold us back. But we have brains and curiosity. **Technology** and our ability to invent have allowed us to go beyond our physical limitations. Inventions have helped us explore the earth. And **innovation** in technology has taken us across land, below water, and up in the skies.

Across Land

Traveling across a continent isn't enough. We want to do it quickly. The first European settlers to cross North America walked for thousands of miles. They used mules or oxen to pull their belongings in wagons.

When the transcontinental railroad was completed in 1869, people could travel from New York to San Francisco. This trip once took six months. Now it could be completed in a week.

What would those travelers think of the innovation of a bullet train? These trains can reach speeds above 322 kilometers per hour (200 miles per hour). The train's car design and the track allow it to move quickly. Engineers took inspiration from the beak of a kingfisher bird for the train's efficient design and shape of the front of the train.

Japanese Shinkansen trains began service across rail lines in 1964. Travel speeds increased from 210 km/h (130 mph) up to 300 km/h (185 mph) today. Future bullet train developments will include running on Maglev (magnetic levitation) rails. Maglev technology allows for speeds of about 482 km/h (300 mph) or more.

English engineer George Stephenson won an English railway competition in 1829 with this locomotive. *The Rocket* carried 30 passengers at about 48 kilometers per hour (30 miles per hour).

The Union Pacific's *Big Boys* were among the largest locomotives ever made. They were built in the late 1930s. By 1961, they were all out of service.

In 1934 the stainless-steel, diesel-electric Burlington *Zephyr* made a dawn-to-dusk trip from Denver, CO, to Chicago, IL. It surpassed every speed record of the time. It averaged about 124 km/h (77 mph) and traveled as fast as 180 km/h (112 mph) along the way.

AMBITIOUS JAPAN!

Below Water

People have always been able to swim, and they have probably wanted to swim deep in the ocean. The mysterious deep waters of the ocean excite the human imagination. What might we find at the bottom of the sea? And what animals might live in this dark place?

People cannot safely swim to the bottom of the ocean, so they are limited to how deep they can dive. Self-contained underwater breathing apparatus (SCUBA) equipment allows people to dive deeper than they can without it.

Even with SCUBA equipment, people cannot dive to the deepest point in the ocean. At the very bottom of the ocean, the pressure is 1,000 times greater than at sea level. Scientists continue to develop machines that can work under this great pressure. Some machines are remotely operated. Others carry humans. We learn more about the ocean's depths with each deep dive.

As technology develops, underwater dives are not only about diving deeply. Scientists consider how long a vessel can stay beneath the water. They set goals for what a dive team can accomplish while aboard. The *Jialong* is a Chinese deep-diving submarine. It is named after a mythical sea dragon. The vessel is designed to reach depths of about 7 kilometers (4 miles/21,120 feet).

The first attempt to reach the bottom of the ocean was made in the unpowered *Bathysphere*. American engineer, Otis Barton, built it. In 1932, he and naturalist William Beebe successfully reached a depth of 923 meters (3,028 feet) in the *Bathysphere*.

Swiss scientist Auguste Piccard along with his son, Jacques, created the bathyscaphe *Trieste*. The Challenger Deep of the Mariana Trench in the Pacific Ocean is the deepest point on Earth. In 1960, Jacques and U.S. Navy Lt. Don Walsh descended into the Trench. They touched bottom at 10,915 meters (35,810 feet).

The robot *Nereus*, named for the Greek sea god, made an extremely deep dive. It submerged to 10,902 meters (35,768 feet) below the surface. People on a ship remotely controlled it.

Up in the Air

Flight is one of the oldest human dreams. People have always wanted to fly like birds. Ancient mythology shows how people wanted to join the birds in the air. On his deathbed in 1519, the genius Leonardo da Vinci said he wished he had been able to fly.

Through the years, many scientists and engineers tried to fly. Some came closer than others, but controlled flight remained a dream. Then in 1903, two bicycle shop workers, Wilbur and Orville Wright, successfully lifted off.

Since then, flight has become routine. Planes fly around the world every day. But to fly alone, like a bird, is still beyond our reach. But nothing can stop the human spirit. Our ability to engineer new technology will, as always, join with our imaginations. This will open methods of transportation that we cannot imagine today. If people can dream it, they will learn how to build it.

In the early 1780s, French brothers Joseph-Michel and Jacques-Etienne Montgolfier invented the first hot air balloon. Hot air from a fire was blown into a silk balloon attached to a basket. The hot air balloon rose. The balloon flew wherever the wind wanted to take it.

On December 17, 1903, Wilbur and Orville Wright flew 120 feet in 12 seconds. It was the first powered flight for humanity, but it was far from the last. The brothers continued to experiment. Modern aircraft reflects their innovations.

A prize for a human-powered aircraft inspired American Paul MacCready. He designed a very light, aerodynamic plane powered by human motion. In 1977, Bryan Allen pedaled the plane on a figure-eight course. The flight lasted 7 minutes and 27 seconds and reached about 17 kilometers per hour (11 mph).

Swiss pilot and inventor, Yves Rossy leaps from a plane wearing a six-foot wing. It has four tiny jet engines on it. He steers by shifting his body from side to side—and he lands on earth using a parachute.

Check In How does science impact transportation?

ZIPPING AROUND

by Renee Biermann
illustrated by Stephen Gilpin

NARRATOR

BRENNA, female

RIPLEY, male

KENDRA, female

SIDNEY, female

GAVIN, male

INTRODUCTION

SETTING *The play takes place far in the future.* NARRATOR
enters and speaks to the audience to explain this exciting, new world.

NARRATOR: Welcome to the future! What's your prediction about how people live? **Airborne** cars? People using jet packs to zoom around? It's all true. Humans agreed to stay off the earth's surface as much as possible as an experiment to replenish nature and protect animal species. Even though it's all right to go to the ground again, traveling and playing there are things of the past! These days, everyone lives high above ground level in apartment buildings that reach to the clouds. Brenna and Ripley are siblings, and they're moving into their new Super-High, High-Rise home. They don't know that a surprise from the past awaits them!

ACT 1

[**SETTING** *In the Super-High, High-Rise, BRENNA, RIPLEY, KENDRA, SIDNEY, and GAVIN are sitting in the living room. They are surrounded by moving boxes and furniture that has just arrived.*]

SIDNEY: I love your new apartment, guys! You're going to be so much closer to all of us now.

RIPLEY: I know! I'm glad we won't have to take two different air-buses to get to school anymore.

BRENNA: And now we get our own rooms, which is good because I was getting tired of listening to Ripley snore.

[RIPLEY *glares at* BRENNA.]

GAVIN: What should we do today? Do you want to zoom to the new FlyPlex?

KENDRA: [*annoyed*] We always go to the FlyPlex, and it's boring!

SIDNEY: No, it's not. We always have a good time, and I even brought my new jet pack!

RIPLEY: [*interrupting*] Wait, you guys. We can't do anything fun today.

BRENNA: [*sighs*] Yeah, sorry. Our Mom says we have to clean out the storage unit that comes with the apartment. It's one of our chores.

GAVIN: There are five of us. We can get it done quickly, and then we can all go to the FlyPlex. [*looks at KENDRA*]

KENDRA: [*shakes head and smiles*] Fine, fine. Let's clean it out, and then we can go.

ACT 2

[**SETTING** *Brenna and Ripley's Mom opens the door to the storage unit for their apartment. The room is filled with boxes and items from the past. BRENNA, RIPLEY, KENDRA, SIDNEY, and GAVIN enter. They all look confused by what they see.*]

KENDRA: What IS all of this stuff? [*picks up the pair of soccer cleats and examines the soles*] Why would anyone wear shoes with pegs on the bottom?

RIPLEY: [*shrugs shoulders*] We don't know what any of it is.

BRENNA: That's why we have to clean it out—it's just old junk.

[KENDRA *throws the soccer cleats back into their shoe box and into the garbage can.* GAVIN *and* SIDNEY *begin picking up items to throw away.* RIPLEY *wanders over to look at a big box in the corner. On the side of the box, there are two words:* DOUBLE ZIPP.]

RIPLEY: [*excited*] Hey, look at this! Have you ever heard of a DOUBLE ZIPP?

[BRENNA, KENDRA, GAVIN, *and* SIDNEY *gather around the box. They all mumble, "No," or shake their heads to show they don't recognize the name.*]

GAVIN: [*curious*] Let's leave that until last, and then we can figure it out.

BRENNA: Good idea, Gavin. Let's get to work.

ACT 3

[**SETTING** *Still in the storage room. Everything is gone except the pieces of the DOUBLE ZIPP.*]

SIDNEY: There are images here that show how to put this thing together, but there aren't any words except, "Get moving on your DOUBLE ZIPP. It's twice the fun."

GAVIN: [*worried*] Do you think we can figure it out?

RIPLEY: [*confident*] Sure, we can. We're **innovative**, right? Let's just start at the beginning and go from there.

[*Characters begin to put together the mystery structure.*]

BRENNA: This is actually kind of fun.

KENDRA: I think it must have been used as a way to travel. I have a hologram of my great-great-great-grandma sitting on an old vehicle that was built from past **technology.** The photo was taken way back when people lived in buildings that started on ground level and only went up to about 30 floors or so. They called them "High Rises."

BRENNA: Ha! That's hilarious. So strange. Well, maybe this was a vehicle.

[*Lights fade. Characters freeze as NARRATOR enters the scene.*]

NARRATOR: The group of friends worked for hours to piece together the mysterious DOUBLE ZIPP. They thought the completed structure would give them all of the answers, but they were still confused.

[NARRATOR *exits. Lights up. The DOUBLE ZIPP has been assembled. It's a double-seated tandem bicycle. All characters look even more confused.*]

GAVIN: [*irritated*] I guess we failed the "**transportation** experiment." What are we going to do with THAT?

RIPLEY: [*sighs*] I really don't know.

BRENNA: [*sits on back bumper of DOUBLE ZIPP and tries to make it move, looks bewildered*] I wish we could travel back in time to ask your great-great-great grandma what people did with things like this. It looks cool, but I don't understand it.

SIDNEY: [*pulls crumpled piece of paper out of the DOUBLE ZIPP box, excited*] Wait a minute! There is one page left in the box. Look at this! It's a picture of people using the DOUBLE ZIPP!

[*Characters gather around to look at the piece of paper. They seem to now understand what the DOUBLE ZIPP is for.*]

KENDRA: This kind of technology moves on the ground.

GAVIN: The ground? No one goes to the ground! I don't know if we can fly that low.

RIPLEY: I heard people used to use paths along the ground before everyone went airborne. Look at the picture closely . . .

ACT 4

BRENNA: [*happy*] I've never been down here before. My parents said they flew down once or twice before we were born. It's actually kind of pretty.

GAVIN: I know what you mean. Look at all of these bugs and plants! And it feels good to be on solid ground! [*jumps up and down on path*]

[*Characters all look around with amazement.*]

KENDRA: Let's try out the DOUBLE ZIPP. In the picture, two people were sitting on it.

[*RIPLEY and GAVIN sit on the DOUBLE ZIPP seats.*]

RIPLEY: What do we do now? I'm not sure what to do with myself if I'm not in the Human Fly Zone.

[*Everyone laughs.*]

[*Characters freeze. NARRATOR enters scene.*]

NARRATOR: [*amused*] Certainly, anyone from the past would know exactly what to do with the DOUBLE ZIPP, but our story is in the future. The key is to use the pedals together at the same time. Poor RIPLEY and GAVIN first tried pedaling in the opposite directions, so they didn't move at all. But they kept trying again and again, and finally they got the old bicycle to work!

[NARRATOR *exits. Characters* unfreeze.] [RIPLEY *and* GAVIN *are riding the bicycle together. They are surprised and excited.*]

GAVIN: This is great!

RIPLEY: I never imagined we'd have so much fun on this crazy, old thing that can't even go airborne!

BRENNA: That looks so exciting. Let me try!

KENDRA: Yeah! Come back here, boys!

SIDNEY: We can all take turns. We have the whole rest of the day to play with the DOUBLE ZIPP, and this will be way more fun than the Flyplex!

KENDRA: I agree!

[*Characters freeze. NARRATOR enters scene.*]

NARRATOR: As the day progressed, more and more people came to see the DOUBLE ZIPP. Cars and air-buses flew low, so the passengers could see what was happening on the ground. The news spread quickly, and more friends came to join Ripley, Kendra, Brenna, Gavin, and Sidney.

[*NARRATOR exits. Characters unfreeze. They all stand together with the DOUBLE ZIPP. They are tired after a long day of riding.*]

GAVIN: I can't believe that people gave up this method of transportation. With a little practice, I bet you could move pretty quickly!

BRENNA: Well, now we've brought it out into the world again.

RIPLEY: And I thought it might only be a flying chair! Brenna and I probably would've just thrown it away while we were cleaning.

KENDRA: These wheels are something else! Let's go around again. I want to really zip this time, right into the future!

[*All characters look happy and one takes out a really small hand-held device and snaps a picture.*]

Check In How is transportation in this play different from today?

Discuss | Ideas in Texts

1. What do you think connects the three pieces you read in this book? What makes you think that?

2. How do the diagrams in the first article help you understand differences among modern cars?

3. The first two articles in this book use a comparison text structure. What does each article compare? How are the comparisons in each article alike and different?

4. Summarize what happens in the play.

5. How does the narrator help you understand the events in the play?

6. What questions do you still have about transportation innovations? What do you want to know more about?